Retiring Wisely

A Comprehensive Guide to Planning Your Retirement

Robert M. McNeill

Copyright © 2023 Robert M. McNeill

All rights reserved. No part of this book may be reproduced, distributed, or transmitted in any form or by any means, including photocopying, recording, or other electronic or mechanical methods, without the prior written permission of the publisher, except in the case of brief quotations embodied in critical reviews and certain other noncommercial uses permitted by copyright law.

This book is a copyrighted work and Robert M. McNeill owns all rights in it. No part of this publication may be reproduced, stored in a retrieval system, or transmitted in any form or by any means, electronic, mechanical, photocopying, recording or otherwise, without the prior written permission of the author.

Contents

Introduction
    Explanation
    Importance of planning early
    Understanding the retirement process

Understanding Your financial status
    Budgeting and Tracking Your Expenses
    Assessment of Your Debt and Savings
    Understanding Your Investment Portfolio

Planning for retirement income and Insurance planning
    Pension plans and IRAs
    Insurance planning
    Annuities and life insurance policies
    Investment options and strategies

Social security and medicare
    How social security works
    Eligibility for social security and Medicare
    How to Maximize Your Benefits

Estate planning
    Understanding estate taxes
    Writing a Will and Creating an Estate Plan
    Understanding Power of Attorney and Guardianship

Health considerations in Retirement
    Long-Term Care and Healthcare Costs
    Understanding Medicare Coverage

How to Pay for Healthcare in Retirement

Managing Your Retirement Lifestyle
- Retirement housing options
- Travel and Leisure Planning
- Voluntary Work and Volunteering

Navigating Retirement Challenges
- Dealing with Inflation
- Understanding the Impact of Market Volatility
- Managing Debt in Retirement

Working During Retirement
- Part-Time Jobs and Consulting Work
- Starting a Business
- Maximizing Social Security Benefits While Working

Conclusion
- Final Thoughts on Planning for Retirement
- How to Keep Your Retirement Plan on Track
- Where to Find More Resources and Support

Introduction

Retirement is a stage in life that many people look forward to, but it can also be a source of anxiety if not properly planned for. Whether you are just starting your career or are approaching retirement age, it's never too early or late to start thinking about how you want to spend your golden years. Retirement planning is an essential aspect of financial planning that can help ensure a secure and fulfilling future.

This book is a comprehensive guide to retirement planning that covers all the essential aspects of this crucial financial decision. Whether you are a young professional, a seasoned worker, or a retiree, you will find valuable information and practical advice that will help you achieve your retirement goals. The book provides a comprehensive overview of the different retirement options available, including pensions, Social Security, and individual retirement accounts (IRAs). It covers important topics such as the impact of inflation, taxes, and Social Security on your retirement income and provides tips on how to make your money last throughout retirement.

One of the most important aspects of retirement planning is understanding the importance of saving and investing for the future. The book provides practical tips and strategies on how to save and invest your money so that you can build a nest egg that will provide you with financial security in your golden years. You will learn how to set achievable savings goals and understand the different types of investments that are suitable for retirement planning. In addition to financial planning, the book also covers the non-financial aspects of retirement, including health and wellness, relationships, and personal growth. You will learn how to stay healthy and active in retirement, how to maintain and strengthen your relationships, and how to pursue new interests and activities that bring you joy and fulfillment.

Whether you are just starting to plan for retirement or are already retired, this book provides the information and guidance you need to make the most of your golden years. With its comprehensive and practical approach, this book will help you build a secure and fulfilling retirement that you can look forward to with confidence. So, whether you want to ensure a comfortable retirement, travel the world, or pursue new interests, this book is the essential guide to help you achieve your retirement dreams.

Explanation

What is retirement

Retirement is a stage in life when an individual stops working and receive a retirement income, usually in the form of a pension, Social Security benefits, or personal savings. It is typically associated with a time of transition when people can pursue new interests, travel, spend more time with family and friends, and enjoy a more relaxed pace of life. Retirement is typically considered to begin between the ages of 60 and 70, depending on the individual's circumstances and personal goals. The length of retirement can vary, but it typically lasts several decades, so it is important to plan and ensure that you have enough financial resources to maintain your lifestyle throughout retirement.

Retirement is a stage in life that most of us dream of, but it can also be a source of worry and stress if not properly planned. The truth is, with proper retirement planning, you can ensure that you have enough financial resources to maintain your lifestyle, enjoy your golden years, and have peace of mind. The good news is that, no matter what stage of life you are in, it's never too early or too late to start planning for retirement.

Retirement planning is the process of evaluating your current financial situation, setting goals for retirement, and developing a strategy to achieve those goals. It involves forecasting your expected expenses and income in retirement, estimating the amount of savings you will need, and determining the best ways to save and invest your money. Retirement planning also includes regular monitoring and updating of your plan to ensure that it remains on track as your circumstances and goals change over time.

Retirement planning is an important aspect of financial planning because it helps you ensure that you have enough resources to maintain your standard of living and support your desired lifestyle during retirement. It also helps you plan for unexpected events, such as health issues or changes in the economy, so that you can make adjustments to your plan as needed. By planning and being proactive, you can enjoy a secure and fulfilling retirement.

Retirement planning helps you understand how much money you will need in retirement and how to best save and invest your money to reach those goals. Here are some key elements of retirement planning that you should be aware of:

Evaluate Your Current Financial Situation
The first step in retirement planning is to assess your current financial situation. This includes taking inventory of your income, expenses, debts, and assets. Knowing your current financial standing will give you a better idea of how much money you need to save and invest to reach your retirement goals.

Set Retirement Goals
Once you know your current financial situation, you can then start setting retirement goals. This can include how much money you want to have in retirement, what kind of lifestyle you want to maintain, and how long you want your savings to last. It's important to be realistic about your goals and to make adjustments as needed.

Determine Your Retirement Income
The next step is to determine your expected retirement income. This includes considering Social Security benefits, pensions, and any other sources of income. Knowing your expected retirement income

will help you determine if you need to save more or if you are on track to reach your goals.

Plan Your Savings and Investment Strategy
Now that you know your expected retirement income and your goals, it's time to start saving and investing. A good retirement plan includes a balanced investment portfolio that includes stocks, bonds, and other investments that match your risk tolerance and financial goals. You should also consider factors such as taxes, inflation, and market fluctuations when planning your investment strategy.

Regularly Review and Update Your Plan
Retirement planning is not a one-time event. It's important to regularly review and update your plan as your circumstances and goals change. You should reassess your plan every year or when there is a significant life change, such as getting married, having children, or changing jobs.

Retirement planning is not only about securing your financial future but also about ensuring a fulfilling and enjoyable retirement. By planning and preparing for retirement, you can ensure that you have the financial resources to maintain your lifestyle, pursue new interests, and enjoy your golden years with peace of mind. So, whether you are just starting your career or are nearing retirement age, take the time to start planning for your future today. Your future self will thank you.

Importance of planning early

Planning for retirement early is essential for ensuring a secure and comfortable lifestyle in your golden years. Retirement planning can seem like a daunting task, but it's important to start early and make sure you're making the right decisions for your future. Here are some of the key benefits of planning for retirement early.

It gives you more time to save: By starting to save and invest early, you have more time to compound your money through compounding interest and take advantage of the power of compounding. This means that money saved in your early years earns you more money over time. Starting early also allows you to save more overall, as you have more time to build up your retirement nest egg.

You can take advantage of tax benefits: Contributing to a retirement account, such as a 401(k), allows you to take advantage of tax-deferred growth. This means that you don't have to pay taxes on your contributions or the growth on your investments until you withdraw money in retirement. This can help you save more money overall and reduce your tax bill in retirement.

You can plan for a longer retirement: The average life expectancy is increasing, which means that many people are living longer in retirement. Planning for a longer retirement means saving more money to ensure that you have enough to last you through your golden years. By starting early, you can save more money and have a more secure retirement.

You can have better control over your retirement: By planning and investing early, you have more control over the type of retirement you want to have. You can decide how much risk you want to take with your investments and determine the best retirement strategies for your goals. You also have more time to adjust your investments as your goals, needs, and circumstances change.

You can reduce stress: Planning for retirement early can reduce stress, as you have more time to make sure you're making the right decisions for your retirement. This can help you feel more secure in your retirement and give you peace of mind that your finances are in order.

Overall, planning for retirement early is essential for ensuring a secure and comfortable lifestyle in your golden years. Starting early allows you to take advantage of compounding interest, tax benefits, and better control over your retirement plans. It also helps you save more money and reduce stress, so you can enjoy your retirement with peace of mind.

Understanding the retirement process

Retirement is an important milestone in everyone's life. It marks the end of your working life and the beginning of a new journey. While retirement can be a time of excitement and new experiences, it can also be daunting and confusing. Navigating the retirement process can be challenging, and it's important to understand the steps involved. The good news about retirement is that, with proper planning and understanding of the retirement process, you can ensure a secure and fulfilling future.

The retirement process involves several important steps that will help you prepare for and transition into retirement.

The first step in the retirement process is deciding when to retire. This is a personal decision and should be based on your financial situation and lifestyle. You should also consider the impact of retirement on your taxes and Social Security benefits.

Once you've decided to retire, you'll need to apply for Social Security benefits. You can apply online or in person at your local Social Security office. When you apply, you'll need to provide proof of your age and earnings, as well as information about your current and past employers.

The next step is to open a retirement account. This will be your primary source of income once you stop working. There are several different types of retirement accounts, including 401(k)s, IRAs, and annuities. It's important to research the different options and choose one that best fits your needs.

Once you've opened a retirement account, you'll need to decide how to invest your money. You should consider your risk tolerance and investment goals when making this decision. It's also important to understand the costs associated with investing, such as fees and taxes.

You'll need to make a plan for how to spend your retirement. This should include budgeting for expenses, setting goals, and planning for the future. If you need help, you can consult a financial advisor or take a class on retirement planning.

Understanding the retirement process can help you make informed decisions and prepare for the next phase of your life. By taking the time to research your options and understand the process, you can ensure that your retirement years are enjoyable and rewarding.

Here's a guide to help you better understand the retirement process:

Evaluate Your Current Financial Situation

The next step in the retirement process is to assess your current financial situation. This includes taking inventory of your income, expenses, debts, and assets. Knowing your current financial standing will give you a better idea of how much money you need to save and invest to reach your retirement goals.

Set Retirement Goals

Once you know your current financial situation, you can then start setting retirement goals. This can include how much money you want to have in retirement, what kind of lifestyle you want to maintain, and how long you want your savings to last. It's important to be realistic about your goals and to make adjustments as needed.

Determine Your Retirement Income

The next step is to determine your expected retirement income. This includes considering Social Security benefits, pensions, and any other sources of income. Knowing your expected retirement income will help you determine if you need to save more or if you are on track to reach your goals.

Plan Your Savings and Investment Strategy

Now that you know your expected retirement income and your goals, it's time to start saving and investing. A good retirement plan includes a balanced investment portfolio that includes stocks, bonds, and other investments that match your risk tolerance and financial goals. You should also consider factors such as taxes, inflation, and market fluctuations when planning your investment strategy.

Regularly Review and Update Your Plan

Retirement planning is not a one-time event. It's important to regularly review and update your plan as your circumstances and goals change. You should reassess your plan every year or when there is a significant life change, such as getting married, having children, or changing jobs.

Transitioning into Retirement

Once you reach retirement age, it's time to transition into retirement. This can involve making decisions about your retirement income sources, when to start receiving Social Security benefits, and when to start accessing your retirement savings. It's important to consult with a financial advisor to ensure that you make informed decisions that are in line with your goals and financial situation.

Enjoying Your Retirement

The last step in the retirement process is to enjoy your retirement. This is the time to pursue your interests, travel, spend time with family and friends, and enjoy a more relaxed pace of life.

The retirement process is an exciting and significant milestone in life, but it's important to plan and be proactive to ensure a secure and fulfilling future. By understanding the steps involved in the retirement process, you can take control of your financial future and enjoy the retirement you've always dreamed of.

Understanding Your financial status

Retirement planning is a complex and ongoing process, but it all starts with understanding your current financial situation. Knowing your current financial standing is the first step in planning for a secure and fulfilling retirement.

Here's a guide to help you understand your current financial situation and get started with retirement planning:

Assess Your Income and Expenses
The first step in understanding your current financial situation is to assess your income and expenses. This includes taking a close look at your monthly bills, debt payments, and any other regular expenses. You should also consider any irregular expenses, such as home repairs or medical bills. Knowing your income and expenses will give you a better idea of how much money you have available to save and invest for retirement.

Review Your Debt

Next, you should review your debt, including any mortgages, car loans, credit card balances, and other debts. It's important to have a clear understanding of your debt obligations and to prioritize paying off high-interest debt, such as credit cards, as soon as possible. This will free up more money to save for retirement and help you reach your goals more quickly.

Evaluate Your Assets

In addition to your income and expenses, it's important to evaluate your assets, including savings accounts, investments, and retirement accounts. You should also consider any other assets, such as real estate or a business, that you may have. Knowing your assets will give you a better idea of your net worth and help you determine how much you need to save and invest to reach your retirement goals.

Plan for Unexpected Expenses

It's also important to plan for unexpected expenses, such as health issues, job loss, or other financial emergencies. Having a savings account specifically designated for emergencies can help you stay on track with your retirement plan, even if unexpected expenses arise.

Consult a Financial Advisor

Finally, it's a good idea to consult a financial advisor. A financial advisor can help you assess your current financial situation, set retirement goals, and develop a plan to reach those goals. They can also help you stay on track and make adjustments as needed over time.

Understanding your current financial situation is a crucial step in retirement planning. By assessing your income, expenses, debt, and assets, you can get a clear picture of your financial situation and develop a plan to reach your retirement goals. With the help of a financial advisor, you can ensure a secure and fulfilling retirement.

You could also follow the steps below

Knowing how much income you have, how much you have saved, and how much you need to save each month can help you determine what kind of retirement plan is best for you. It can also help you decide when to begin saving and how much to save each month.

Understanding your current financial status is to assess your income and expenses. Take a look at your current income sources, such as wages, investments, Social Security, and other income. Then, account for your expenses, like rent or mortgage payments, utilities, insurance premiums, and other bills. This will give you a clearer picture of your current financial situation and how much you need to save each month to meet your retirement goals.

You will also need to evaluate your current investments. This includes looking at your retirement accounts, such as 401(k)s and IRAs, as well as any other investments you've made. This can help you determine whether or not you are on track for retirement and if you need to make any adjustments to your savings plan.

It is also very important to understand your risk tolerance. Retirement planning involves making decisions about how much risk you are willing to take on and what type of investments you're comfortable making. Knowing your risk tolerance will help you make sound decisions when it comes to investing your retirement funds.

Understanding your financial status is essential for making the best decisions when it comes to retirement planning. Taking the time to assess your income and expenses, evaluate your investments, and understand your risk tolerance will help you create a retirement plan that meets your needs and goals.

Budgeting and Tracking Your Expenses

Budgeting and tracking your expenses are two essential tools for successful retirement planning. These tools will help you understand where your money is going and make informed decisions about how to allocate your resources.

Here's a guide to help you start budgeting and tracking your expenses:

Create a Budget

The first step in budgeting is to create a budget. This involves listing your income and expenses and determining how much money you have available to save and invest for retirement. A budget will help you identify areas where you can reduce your expenses and allocate more money toward retirement savings.

Track Your Expenses

Once you have a budget, the next step is to track your expenses. This involves keeping a record of your spending and comparing it to your budget. Tracking your expenses will help you stay on track with your budget and identify areas where you may need to make changes.

Use Budgeting Tools
There are many tools available to help you budget and track your expenses, such as personal finance software, apps, or a simple spreadsheet. Using these tools can make the process easier and help you stay organized.

Review and Adjust Your Budget Regularly
It's important to review and adjust your budget regularly. This will help you stay on track with your retirement goals and make changes as your circumstances change. For example, if you receive a raise or incur new expenses, you may need to adjust your budget to reflect these changes.

Be Realistic

When creating a budget, it's important to be realistic. Set achievable goals and be honest with yourself about your spending habits. Remember that budgeting and tracking your expenses are not meant to restrict your spending, but to help you make informed decisions about your finances.

You should also ensure that you are putting enough money into your retirement plans. Many employers offer retirement plans, such as 401(k)s, that allow you to save money on a tax-deferred basis. Make sure to contribute as much as you can afford to these plans to ensure that you have a comfortable retirement.

Budgeting and tracking your expenses are key components of retirement planning. By understanding your income and expenses, you can make informed decisions about how to allocate your resources and reach your retirement goals. With the help of budgeting tools and a little discipline, you can ensure a secure and fulfilling retirement.

Assessment of Your Debt and Savings

Having a good assessment of your debt and savings can help you make better decisions for your financial future. Knowing what you owe and what you have saved will help you plan for retirement and other financial goals. Here is how to assess your debt and savings.

Debt Assessment

The first step in assessing your debt is to identify the different types of debt you have. Examples of debt include mortgages, car loans, student loans, credit cards, and other types of financial obligations. Write down the total amount you owe for each type of debt, the interest rate, and the minimum monthly payment.

Once you have a clear picture of the debt you owe, it's time to evaluate your debt-to-income ratio. This ratio measures the amount of your gross income that is devoted to debt payments. Divide your total debt payments by your gross income to get your debt-to-income ratio.

If your debt-to-income ratio is too high, you may want to consider ways to reduce your debt. You could start by making more than the minimum payments on your debts. You could also negotiate with creditors to lower the interest rate on your debts.

Savings Assessment

To assess your savings, you need to determine how much you have saved and how much you should be saving. Start by calculating how much money you have saved in retirement accounts, savings accounts, and other investments. Add up the total amount of all your savings and investments.

Next, consider how much of your income you should be saving for retirement. A good rule of thumb is to save 15% of your gross income for retirement. So, if you make $50,000 a year, you should aim to save $7,500 for retirement.

Consider how you can increase your savings. You could start by setting up an automatic transfer from your checking account to your savings account each month. You could also look for ways to save money on your taxes, such as contributing to a retirement account or taking advantage of tax credits.

Assessing your debt and savings is an important step in managing your finances. Knowing what you owe and what you have saved will help you make better decisions for your financial future. Take the time to evaluate your debt and savings, and you will be on your way to achieving your financial goals.

Understanding Your Investment Portfolio

For many, managing a retirement portfolio is a daunting task – and it's understandable why. There is a lot to consider when deciding how to invest your hard-earned money for retirement. It can be difficult to know where to start and what strategies to use.

However, having a thorough understanding of your retirement portfolio is essential for your long-term financial success and peace of mind. In this article, we will take a look at the basics of understanding and managing your retirement portfolio, as well as tips on how to make the most of your investments.

First, it's important to understand the different types of investments that are available to you. Generally, retirement portfolios are composed of stocks, bonds, mutual funds, and cash equivalents. Each type of investment carries its level of risk, so it's important to consider your risk tolerance and goals when selecting your investments.

Next, you'll want to determine the asset allocation of your portfolio. Asset allocation is the process of dividing your portfolio into different asset classes, such as stocks, bonds, and cash equivalents. Diversifying your investments is important for minimizing risk, as different asset classes have different levels of risk.

It's important to consider the tax implications of your investments. Many retirement accounts are tax-advantaged, meaning that you can benefit from tax-free growth or deferral of taxes until you withdraw the funds. Be sure to research the tax implications of each type of investment you are considering.

It's important to review your portfolio regularly. Make sure that your investments are still aligned with your risk tolerance and goals, and that they are performing as expected. If not, it may be time to rebalance your portfolio to ensure that you are staying on track with your long-term goals.

It's also good to consider consulting a financial advisor. A financial advisor can help you assess your debt and savings, set goals, and develop a plan to reach those goals. They can also help you stay on track and make adjustments as needed over time.

Understanding and managing your retirement portfolio can seem intimidating, but it doesn't have to be. With a little bit of knowledge and research, you can make informed decisions about your investments that will help you reach your financial goals. With the help of a financial advisor, you can ensure a secure and fulfilling retirement.

Planning for retirement income and Insurance planning

Planning for retirement income is an important aspect of financial planning that should not be overlooked. Retirement income refers to the funds that you receive regularly, typically after you have stopped working, to help sustain your lifestyle. Retirement income planning aims to ensure that you have enough funds to support your needs in retirement.

Here are some steps to help you plan for your retirement income:

Determine your expenses: Knowing how much money you need in retirement is crucial in planning for retirement income. Make a budget of your current expenses and adjust it to reflect what you anticipate your expenses will be in retirement. Consider factors such as inflation, healthcare expenses, and travel plans.

Assess your current savings: Review your current savings, including your 401(k), IRA, and any other retirement accounts. Estimate the amount you can expect to receive from these accounts in retirement.

Estimate your Social Security benefits: Social Security provides a monthly income to eligible retirees. Visit the Social Security Administration website to estimate your monthly benefit.

Calculate your retirement income gap: Subtract the estimated amount of money you expect to receive from your retirement savings and Social Security from your estimated retirement expenses. This will give you an idea of the gap you need to fill to achieve your desired retirement lifestyle.

Consider your options for filling the gap: There are various options for filling the retirement income gap, including investing in annuities, taking out a reverse mortgage, or continuing to work part-time. Consider your options and speak with a financial advisor to determine the best strategy for your situation.

Review and adjust your plan regularly: As your circumstances change, you may need to adjust your plan. Regularly reviewing your plan and making adjustments will help ensure that you are on track to achieve your desired retirement lifestyle.

Planning for retirement income is essential to ensure that you have enough funds to support your needs in retirement. Start by determining your expenses, assessing your current savings, and estimating your

Social Security benefits. Fill the gap by considering your options and regularly reviewing your plan. Speak with a financial advisor for personalized advice and guidance.

Pension plans and IRAs

Pension plans and IRAs are two of the most popular retirement savings options for individuals and families. Both offer tax-deferred growth and long-term security, but there are some key differences between them. Knowing these differences can help you decide which option is best for your retirement planning needs.

Pension plans, also known as defined benefit plans, are employer-sponsored retirement savings plans. They are funded by employers and are designed to provide a steady stream of income in retirement. A portion of each employee's salary is put into the plan and employers typically match contributions. When you retire, you receive a set amount of money each month for the rest of your life, regardless of how long you live.

Individual Retirement Accounts (IRAs) are retirement savings plans for individuals and families. They are funded by the individual and are designed to provide an additional source of income in retirement. With an IRA, you can make annual contributions and choose from a variety of investment options. The money grows tax-deferred and you can withdraw it at any time, subject to certain rules and regulations.

Pension plans offer a guaranteed income in retirement, while IRAs offer more flexibility in terms of contributions and investment options. Pension plans are typically funded by employers and offer tax-deferred growth, while IRAs are funded by the individual and offer more control over investments and withdrawals.

When deciding between a pension plan and an IRA, consider your retirement goals, your current income, and your long-term plans. Pension plans can provide a steady stream of income in retirement, while IRAs offer more flexibility in terms of contributions and investment options.

No matter which option you choose, it is important to start saving for retirement as soon as possible. The earlier you start, the more money you will have in retirement. Consider seeking the advice of a financial advisor to help you decide which retirement savings option is best for you.

Insurance planning

Insurance planning is an essential part of retirement planning. It helps to ensure that you and your family have the financial resources to handle unexpected events.

Insurance planning involves understanding the risks associated with retirement and determining the best way to protect yourself and your family from these risks. This can include choosing the right type of insurance, understanding how much coverage is needed, and finding the best rates and coverage.

The first step in insurance planning is to determine your needs. You will need to assess your current financial situation, your goals, and any risks that could impact your future. This could include factors like your health, your job security, and your family situation. This will help you to identify what types of insurance coverage you need and how much coverage you will require.

Once you have determined your insurance needs, you can start shopping for insurance policies. This can involve a comparison of different insurance products and companies to find the coverage that is best for you. It is important to consider the policy's terms and conditions, such as the premium, the deductibles, and the benefits. You may also want to consider purchasing additional coverage, such as a long-term care policy, to ensure that you have adequate coverage for any future needs.

When choosing an insurance policy, it is important to work with a financial advisor or insurance broker. These professionals can help you to understand the different types of insurance products and how they work, as well as help you to make informed decisions about which coverage is right for you. They can also provide you with support and advice throughout the process.

Life insurance is one of the most important types of insurance to consider when planning for retirement. It provides financial resources to your family in the event of your death. It can also be used to provide an income stream to your family if you become disabled.

Long-term care insurance is another type of insurance to consider when planning for retirement. This type of insurance helps to cover the costs of long-term care services, including nursing home and home health care. It can also provide financial support if you become incapacitated and unable to care for yourself.

Disability insurance is another type of insurance to consider when planning for retirement. This type of insurance provides income to you if you are unable to work due to an illness or injury. It can help to replace the lost income and help to maintain your quality of life.

Finally, annuities are another type of insurance to consider when planning for retirement. Annuities provide a steady stream of income during retirement. They are an excellent way to ensure that you have a secure financial future.

Insurance planning is an important part of retirement planning. It is important to understand the risks associated with retirement and to determine the best way to protect yourself and your family from these risks. Life insurance, long-term care insurance, disability insurance, and annuities are all important types of insurance to consider when planning for retirement.

Here are some of the key benefits of insurance planning as part of your retirement planning:

Guaranteed Income: One of the main advantages of insurance policies for retirement planning is the guaranteed income they provide. Insurance policies like annuities can provide a steady and predictable source of income, which is not subject to the fluctuations of the stock market. This makes it a more secure option for retirees who want to ensure a steady income stream.

Estate Planning: Insurance policies can also be used to help transfer wealth to your beneficiaries after you are gone. Life insurance policies, for example, can provide a death benefit to your loved ones, which can help to cover expenses like funeral costs and other debts, as well as provide a source of income for your beneficiaries.

Tax Benefits: Many insurance policies offer tax benefits, which can help to maximize your retirement savings. For example, premiums paid on life insurance policies are generally tax-deductible, while the death benefit is generally tax-free.

Flexibility: Insurance policies can be customized to meet your specific financial needs and goals. For example, you can choose between different annuity options, such as fixed, variable, or indexed annuities, depending on your investment goals and risk tolerance.

Complements other Investments: Insurance policies can be used in conjunction with other retirement investments, such as 401(k)s and IRAs, to help create a well-rounded and comprehensive retirement plan.

Annuities and life insurance policies

Annuities and life insurance policies are two important tools that can help individuals plan for their retirement. Both are financial products that provide financial security and stability in retirement, but they serve different purposes and have distinct features.

Annuities:
An annuity is a contract between an individual and an insurance company. The individual pays a premium in exchange for a guaranteed stream of income during their retirement years. There are two main types of annuities: immediate annuities and deferred annuities.

Immediate annuities provide a guaranteed income stream immediately after the premium is paid. The income received is based on the individual's life expectancy and the amount of the premium paid.

Immediate annuities are ideal for individuals who need to receive an immediate income stream in retirement, such as individuals who are near retirement and have limited retirement savings.

Deferred annuities are similar to savings accounts, with the individual making contributions over time. The individual can either take the accumulated value as a lump sum or convert it into a stream of income in retirement. Deferred annuities come in two forms: fixed annuities and variable annuities. Fixed annuities provide a guaranteed rate of return, while variable annuities allow the individual to invest in a variety of underlying assets, such as stocks and bonds.

Life Insurance Policies:

Life insurance policies are designed to provide financial protection for the policyholder's beneficiaries in the event of their death. In addition to providing death benefits, life insurance policies can also be used as a retirement planning tool. There are two main types of life insurance policies: term life insurance and permanent life insurance.

Term life insurance provides coverage for a specified period, typically 10, 20, or 30 years. If the policyholder dies during the term, the beneficiaries receive a death benefit. Term life insurance is typically less expensive than permanent life insurance, making it a cost-effective option for individuals who want to ensure their beneficiaries receive a death benefit.

Permanent life insurance, such as whole life insurance and universal life insurance, provides coverage for the policyholder's entire life. In addition to death benefits, permanent life insurance policies also have a savings component, which can be used to accumulate wealth for retirement. This component grows tax-deferred and can be used to supplement retirement income.

Annuities and life insurance policies are both valuable tools for individuals who want to plan for their retirement. Annuities provide a guaranteed stream of income, whole life insurance policies provide financial protection for the policyholder's beneficiaries. When considering which option is best for you, consider your individual financial needs, goals, and risk tolerance. It is important to consult with a financial advisor to determine the best strategy for your unique situation.

Investment options and strategies

Investing is an important component of a comprehensive retirement plan. Investment options and strategies can help individuals grow their savings and achieve their financial goals in retirement. However, with a wide range of investment options available, it can be difficult to determine the best strategy for your individual needs.

Here are some common investment options and strategies to consider as part of your retirement plan:
Stocks: Stocks represent ownership in a company and can provide a long-term investment opportunity with the potential for significant growth. Stocks can be a good option for individuals who have a long time horizon and a high tolerance for risk.
Bonds: Bonds are debt securities that provide a fixed income stream to investors. Bonds are generally considered a more conservative investment option compared to stocks, as they are less volatile and offer a lower return potential.
Mutual Funds: Mutual funds are investment vehicles that pool money from multiple investors to purchase a diversified portfolio of stocks, bonds, and other

securities. Mutual funds can provide exposure to a variety of investment options and can help reduce the risk associated with investing in individual stocks.

Exchange-Traded Funds (ETFs): ETFs are similar to mutual funds, but are traded on stock exchanges like individual stocks. ETFs provide exposure to a variety of investment options and can offer a cost-effective way to invest in a diversified portfolio.

Real Estate Investment Trusts (REITs): REITs invest in income-producing real estates properties, such as apartment buildings, office buildings, and shopping centers. REITs can provide exposure to the real estate market and offer a potential source of income in retirement.

Diversification: Diversification is a critical aspect of a comprehensive retirement plan. Diversifying your investments across a range of asset classes and investment types can help reduce risk and increase the potential for long-term growth.

Dollar-Cost Averaging: Dollar-cost averaging is an investment strategy that involves investing a fixed amount of money at regular intervals, regardless of the price of the investment. This strategy can help reduce the impact of market volatility and increase the potential for long-term growth.

Professional advice: Working with a financial advisor can help you understand your individual financial goals and develop a comprehensive investment strategy to achieve them. A financial advisor can guide investment options, risk management, and portfolio diversification.

Investing is an important component of a comprehensive retirement plan. Consider your individual financial goals, risk tolerance, and time horizon when choosing your investment options and strategies. Diversification, dollar-cost averaging, and professional advice are all critical aspects of a successful investment strategy. By investing regularly and following a well-thought-out strategy, you can increase your chances of achieving your financial goals in retirement.

Social security and medicare

Social Security and Medicare are two critical components of the U.S. and every country around the world. retirement plans that help provide financial security for millions of Americans. These programs are designed to help individuals save for their golden years and ensure that they have the necessary resources to support themselves and their families during their retirement.

Social Security is a federal insurance program that provides benefits to eligible individuals who are retired or disabled. It is funded through payroll taxes paid by workers and their employers. Benefits are calculated based on a formula that takes into account the individual's earnings history and the age at which they decide to begin receiving benefits. Eligible individuals can start receiving benefits as early as age 62, but they will receive a reduced monthly benefit if they begin receiving benefits before their full retirement age (which is between 66 and 67, depending on the year they were born).

Medicare is a federal health insurance program that provides coverage to individuals who are 65 years of age or older, as well as certain individuals with disabilities. It is funded through a combination of payroll taxes paid by workers and their employers and premiums paid by Medicare beneficiaries. Medicare is designed to help cover the cost of necessary medical services, including hospitalization, doctor's visits, and prescription drugs.

Both Social Security and Medicare are essential for ensuring financial security during retirement. Social Security provides a guaranteed income that can help support individuals and their families, while Medicare helps cover the cost of medical expenses. However, both programs face challenges in the future, including rising costs and a growing population of eligible beneficiaries. To maintain the solvency of these programs, Congress may need to make changes to the programs in the future.

Social Security and Medicare are critical components of the U.S. retirement plan that help provide financial security for millions of Americans. These programs are designed to help individuals save for their golden years and ensure that they have the necessary resources to support themselves and their families during their retirement. While both programs face challenges, they continue to play an important role in providing financial security for older Americans and should be protected and strengthened for future generations.

How social security works

Social Security is a federal insurance program that provides financial benefits to eligible individuals who are retired or disabled. It is one of the most important components of the U.S. retirement plan, providing a guaranteed income to support millions of Americans during their golden years. Understanding how Social Security works is essential for anyone planning for their retirement.

Social Security is funded through payroll taxes paid by workers and their employers. The amount of Social Security taxes that an individual pays depends on their earnings, and the taxes are collected by the Social Security Administration (SSA). These funds are used to pay benefits to eligible individuals, such as retirees and disabled workers.

Eligibility for Social Security benefits is based on an individual's earnings history. To be eligible, an individual must have earned enough credits, which are earned through working and paying Social

Security taxes. The amount of Social Security benefits an individual is eligible to receive is determined by a formula that takes into account their average earnings over their working years and the age at which they decide to begin receiving benefits.

Individuals can start receiving Social Security benefits as early as age 62, but they will receive a reduced monthly benefit if they begin receiving benefits before their full retirement age (which is between 66 and 67, depending on the year they were born). On the other hand, individuals who choose to delay receiving benefits can receive a higher monthly benefit when they do begin receiving benefits.

Social Security benefits are designed to provide financial support to eligible individuals, but they are not meant to be an individual's sole source of income during retirement. Individuals are encouraged to save for their retirement through other means, such as a 401(k) or an IRA, to ensure that they have the necessary resources to support themselves and their families during their golden years.

Social Security is a federal insurance program that provides financial benefits to eligible individuals who are retired or disabled. It is one of the most important components of the U.S. retirement plan and provides a guaranteed income to support millions of Americans during their golden years. Understanding how Social Security works is essential for anyone planning for their retirement, and individuals are encouraged to save for their retirement through other means in addition to Social Security.

Eligibility for social security and Medicare

Eligibility for these programs is based on factors such as age, work history, and disability status. We will examine the eligibility requirements for Social Security and Medicare.

Social Security eligibility is based on an individual's work history. To be eligible for Social Security benefits, individuals must have earned enough credits, which are based on their taxable income, over their lifetime. As of 2021, individuals earn one credit for each $1,470 in taxable income. In general, individuals need to earn 40 credits, or roughly 10 years of work, to be eligible for Social Security benefits.

In addition to the credit requirements, individuals must also meet certain age requirements to be eligible for Social Security benefits. Eligible individuals can start receiving benefits as early as age 62, but they will receive a reduced monthly benefit if they begin receiving benefits before their full retirement age (which is between 66 and 67, depending on the year they were born). The full retirement age is the age at which an individual is eligible to receive their full Social Security benefit.

Medicare eligibility, on the other hand, is based on age and disability status. Individuals who are 65 years of age or older and U.S. citizens or permanent legal residents are eligible for Medicare. Certain individuals with disabilities, such as those who have been receiving Social Security disability benefits for at least two years, may also be eligible for Medicare. It is important to note that eligibility for Medicare does not automatically mean eligibility for Social Security benefits. Individuals who are eligible for Medicare must also meet the eligibility requirements for Social Security, which are based on their work history and age.

Eligibility for these programs is based on factors such as work history, age, and disability status, and individuals need to understand these requirements to ensure that they can take advantage of these benefits during their retirement years.

How to Maximize Your Benefits

We will be discussing several strategies for maximizing the benefits of Social Security and Medicare. One of the most important factors that can affect your Social Security benefits is the age at which you start receiving them. As mentioned earlier, you can start receiving benefits as early as age 62, but if you begin receiving benefits before your full retirement age, your monthly benefit will be reduced. On the other hand, if you wait until after your full retirement age to start receiving benefits, your monthly benefit will be increased. Deciding when to start receiving Social Security benefits is a personal decision that depends on your circumstances, but it is important to consider the long-term impact of your choice on your overall retirement income.

Another important factor that can affect your Social Security benefits is your earnings history. Social Security benefits are based on a formula that takes into account your average indexed monthly earnings

(AIME), which is a calculation of your highest 35 years of earnings adjusted for inflation. To maximize your Social Security benefits, it is important to work for at least 35 years and to earn as much as you can during your highest earning years.

In addition to maximizing your Social Security benefits, it is also important to consider strategies for maximizing your Medicare benefits. One of the most important strategies is to enroll in Medicare as soon as you become eligible. If you are already receiving Social Security benefits, you will be automatically enrolled in Medicare, but if you are not yet receiving benefits, you will need to take steps to enroll in the program.

Another important strategy for maximizing your Medicare benefits is to understand the different parts of the program and how they work. Medicare comprises four parts: Part A (Hospital Insurance), Part B (Medical Insurance), Part C (Medicare Advantage), and Part D (Prescription Drug Coverage). To get the most out of Medicare, it is important to understand the different coverage options available under each part and choose the one that is right for you.

To maximize your benefits from these programs, it is important to consider factors such as your age, earnings history, and enrollment options. By understanding these factors and taking steps to maximize your benefits, you can ensure that you have the necessary resources to support yourself and your family during your retirement years.

Estate planning

Estate planning is an important aspect of preparing for retirement. It involves organizing your assets and making arrangements for the distribution of those assets after your death. Estate planning can help ensure that your assets are distributed according to your wishes and that your loved ones are taken care of after you are gone. In this article, we will discuss the basics of estate planning and why it is an important part of your retirement plan.

The first step in estate planning is to identify your assets and determine what you would like to happen to those assets after your death. This includes both financial assets, such as bank accounts, stocks, and real estate, as well as personal assets, such as jewelry, artwork, and personal items. It is important to have a clear understanding of your assets and how they will be distributed after your death.

One of the most important tools in estate planning is a will. A will is a legal document that outlines your wishes for the distribution of your assets after your death. It is important to have a will in place because, without one, the distribution of your assets will be determined by state law, which may not reflect your wishes. A will can also be used to name a guardian for minor children and to designate an executor to manage the distribution of your assets.

Another important aspect of estate planning is estate tax planning. Estate taxes are a tax on the transfer of property after death, and the amount of the tax can be substantial. Estate tax planning can help reduce or eliminate the amount of estate taxes owed by taking advantage of various tax laws and exemptions.

Trusts are another important tool in estate planning. There are many different types of trusts, including revocable trusts, irrevocable trusts, and charitable trusts, and each serves a different purpose. Trusts can be used to hold and manage assets, provide for loved ones after your death, reduce estate taxes, and many other purposes.

In addition to the above, it is also important to consider life insurance in your estate plan. Life insurance can provide a tax-free source of income for your loved ones after your death and can also help pay for final expenses, such as funeral costs and estate taxes.

Understanding estate taxes

Estate taxes can have a significant impact on the distribution of your assets after death. Understanding estate taxes is an important part of estate planning, particularly for those who have a significant amount of assets.

Estate taxes are a tax on the transfer of property after death. The amount of the tax is based on the value of the estate and can be substantial. Estate taxes are levied by the federal government and by some states, so the amount of the tax will vary depending on where you live.

The first step in understanding estate taxes is to determine the value of your estate. Your estate includes all of your assets, including bank accounts, stocks, real estate, personal items, and any other assets that you own. The value of your estate is used to determine the amount of estate taxes owed.

It is important to note that there are exemptions and deductions available that can reduce the amount of estate taxes owed. For example, the federal estate tax exemption is $11.7 million for individuals and $23.4 million for couples in 2021. This means that the first $11.7 million of an individual's estate is exempt from estate taxes, and the first $23.4 million of a couple's estate is exempt from estate taxes. In addition, there are deductions available for certain types of property, such as family-owned farms, and charitable donations.

Another important aspect of estate taxes is that they can be minimized or eliminated through estate tax planning. Estate tax planning involves taking advantage of tax laws and exemptions to reduce or eliminate the amount of estate taxes owed. This can be done through a variety of strategies, such as creating trusts, making gifts, and taking advantage of life insurance.

Writing a Will and Creating an Estate Plan

You need to consider many factors when making a will and creating an estate plan. Here we will discuss the key steps to follow when writing a will and creating an estate plan.

The first step in writing a will is to consider the assets that you own. This includes any real estate, investments, bank accounts, personal property, and life insurance policies. You will need to list out all of your assets and their estimated values. You will also need to list the names and contact information of any beneficiaries you wish to include in your will. The next step is to make decisions about who will be your executor. The executor is the person who will be responsible for carrying out your wishes after your death. You will need to choose someone who is trustworthy and has the ability to manage your estate.

The third step is to decide how you want to distribute your assets. You will need to decide who will receive what assets, and how much each person will receive. It is important to be very specific in the language used in the will.

The fourth step is to designate someone to serve as a guardian for any minor children. This will ensure that your children are taken care of in the event of your death.

The fifth step is to create a retirement plan. This will help ensure that your assets are protected after your death. You should include information about how your assets will be managed, who will have access to them, and how the funds will be distributed.

The sixth step is to create a list of debts and other financial obligations. This will help ensure that your debts are paid off after your death.

The seventh step is to make arrangements for your funeral. You will need to decide who will be responsible for your funeral expenses and how you would like to be remembered.

The eighth step is to make sure that your will is properly executed. You will need to sign and date the will in the presence of two witnesses.

Finally, you will need to make sure that your will is properly filed with the court. This will ensure that your wishes are legally binding and enforceable.

Writing a will and creating an estate plan can seem overwhelming. However, it is important to take the time to make sure that your wishes are carried out after your death. By following these steps, you can ensure that your assets are properly distributed and your loved ones are taken care of.

Understanding Power of Attorney and Guardianship

Power of attorney and guardianship are two important legal concepts that play a crucial role in estate planning. Both concepts involve appointing someone to act on your behalf and make decisions for you if you become unable to do so.

Understanding the differences between the power of attorney and guardianship can help you make informed decisions about who to appoint and when to use these legal tools in your estate plan.

Power of attorney is a legal document that allows you to appoint someone to make decisions on your behalf. There are two main types of power of attorney: durable and springing. A durable power of attorney takes effect immediately and remains in effect even if you become incapacitated while a springing power of attorney only takes effect if you become incapacitated.

With power of attorney, you can appoint someone to make financial and legal decisions on your behalf, such as paying bills, managing investments, and making real estate transactions. Power of attorney can be limited to specific tasks or can be broad in scope, giving the person you appoint a wide range of authority to make decisions on your behalf.

For example, let's say you are a wealthy individual who owns several properties, stocks, and other assets. In the event of your incapacity, you can appoint a trusted person with a durable power of attorney to manage your financial affairs and make decisions on your behalf. This can help ensure that your assets are managed in a way that aligns with your wishes and helps avoid any disputes or confusion.

Guardianship, on the other hand, is a legal arrangement that is used to manage the affairs of individuals who are unable to do so for themselves. Guardianship can be appointed for minors, for individuals who are mentally or physically incapacitated, or for individuals who are unable to make informed decisions.

For example, if you have a minor child or a dependent adult who is unable to make decisions for themselves, you can appoint a guardian to make decisions about their health, finances, and living arrangements. Guardianship is usually appointed by a court and requires a legal process, while power of attorney can be appointed by the individual and does not require court approval.

Health considerations in Retirement

Retirement is a time in your life when you can focus on your health, enjoy your hobbies, and spend time with loved ones. However, retirement also comes with new health considerations that you need to be aware of to ensure that you have a healthy and happy retirement.

Here are some of the most important health considerations to keep in mind as you plan for retirement:

1. Health insurance coverage: As you transition from working to retirement, it is important to make sure that you have adequate health insurance coverage. Medicare is a federal health insurance program for people over 65 years of age, but it may not cover all of your medical expenses. You may also consider purchasing a supplementary Medicare policy or a private health insurance policy.

2. Long-term care: Long-term care refers to the assistance you may need with activities of daily living, such as bathing, dressing, and eating. It is important to consider the cost of long-term care, as it can be expensive, and to plan accordingly. You

may consider purchasing long-term care insurance to help cover the cost of care.

3. Regular check-ups: Regular check-ups with your doctor are important to maintain your health and catch any health issues early on. Regular check-ups can also help you stay on top of your medications, manage any chronic conditions, and receive preventive screenings.

4. Physical activity: Regular physical activity is important for maintaining your health, and it can also help you stay active and engaged as you age. Physical activity can include activities like walking, yoga, swimming, or playing golf. You may also consider joining a fitness center or taking up a new physical activity, like dancing.

5. Nutrition: Eating a healthy and balanced diet is important for maintaining your health, especially as you age. Eating a variety of healthy foods can help you stay active, maintain a healthy weight, and prevent chronic conditions such as heart disease and diabetes.

6. Mental health: Mental health is an important aspect of overall health and wellness, and it is important to take care of your mental health as you age. You may consider seeking help from a mental health professional, joining a support group, or engaging in activities that bring you joy and fulfillment.

Long-Term Care and Healthcare Costs

Long-term care is one of the largest healthcare expenses that people face in retirement, and it is important to plan for this cost in advance. We will discuss long-term care and healthcare costs, and provide tips on how to plan for these costs in your retirement plan.

Long-term care: Long-term care refers to the assistance that people need with activities of daily living, such as bathing, dressing, and eating. This type of care can be provided in a nursing home, assisted living facility, or in your own home. Long-term care can be expensive, and the costs can quickly add up. According to the Genworth Cost of

Care Survey, the median cost of a private room in a nursing home is over $100,000 per year.

Healthcare costs: In addition to long-term care, there are many other healthcare costs that people face in retirement, including doctor visits, hospital stays, prescription drugs, and other medical expenses. These costs can be substantial, and they can eat into your retirement savings if you are not prepared.

Planning for long-term care and healthcare costs: There are several ways to plan for long-term care and healthcare costs in your retirement plan. One option is to purchase long-term care insurance, which can help cover the cost of care if you need it. Another option is to save for these costs in advance, by setting aside money in a dedicated health savings account or by investing in a product designed to help you save for healthcare costs in retirement.

Medicare: Medicare is a federal health insurance program for people over 65 years of age, and it can help cover some of the costs of long-term care and other healthcare expenses. However, Medicare does not cover all of the costs, and you may need to purchase additional insurance or pay out-of-pocket for some expenses.

Medicaid: Medicaid is a joint federal-state program that can help pay for long-term care for people with limited financial resources. To be eligible for Medicaid, you must meet certain financial and eligibility criteria.

Estate planning: Estate planning is an important aspect of retirement planning, and it can help you protect your assets and ensure that they are passed on to your loved ones in the way that you wish. Estate planning can also help you plan for the cost of long-term care and other healthcare expenses, and it can provide peace of mind knowing that your wishes will be followed.

Understanding Medicare Coverage

Tips for making the most of your Medicare benefits.

Parts of Medicare: Medicare is divided into four parts: Part A (hospital insurance), Part B (medical insurance), Part C (Medicare Advantage plans), and Part D (prescription drug coverage). Each part covers different types of healthcare services, and you may choose to enroll in one or more parts, depending on your needs.

Part A: Part A covers inpatient hospital care, skilled nursing facility care, hospice care, and home health care. This coverage is generally free, as most people have paid into the Medicare system through payroll taxes while they were working.

Part B: Part B covers physician services, outpatient care, home health care, and other medical services. You must pay a monthly premium for Part B coverage, and there may be deductibles, coinsurance, or copayments for certain services.

Part C: Part C, also known as Medicare Advantage, is a type of Medicare health plan offered by private insurance companies. Medicare Advantage plans must provide the same benefits as original Medicare (Parts A and B), but they may also offer additional benefits, such as prescription drug coverage, vision, and dental.

Part D: Part D is prescription drug coverage. You can enroll in a standalone Part D plan or choose a Medicare Advantage plan that includes prescription drug coverage.

Cost-sharing: Medicare has various cost-sharing requirements, including premiums, deductibles, coinsurance, and copayments. These costs can add up, and it's important to understand what you'll be responsible for paying.

Coverage limitations: While Medicare covers many healthcare services, it does not cover everything. For example, Medicare does not cover long-term care or cosmetic surgery. It's important to understand what Medicare covers and what it doesn't so that you can plan for any gaps in coverage.

Enrolling in Medicare: Most people become eligible for Medicare when they turn 65, and they can enroll during a seven-month period that begins three months before their 65th birthday and ends three months after. It's important to enroll in Medicare when you're first eligible, as your premium for Part B coverage may be higher if you enroll later.

How to Pay for Healthcare in Retirement

Healthcare costs can be a significant expense in retirement, and it's important to plan for these costs in advance. We'll provide a brief overview of some of the options available to pay for healthcare in retirement, although most of these options have been mentioned previously let's go through it again.

Medicare: Medicare is a federal health insurance program that provides coverage for people over 65 years of age and certain younger people with disabilities. Medicare covers a wide range of healthcare services, but it does not cover everything, and there may be deductibles, coinsurance, and copayments for certain services. To make the most of your Medicare benefits, it's important to understand what Medicare covers and what it doesn't.

Medicare Supplement Insurance: Medicare Supplement Insurance, also known as Medigap, can help cover some of the out-of-pocket costs that Medicare does not cover. Medigap plans are sold by private insurance companies, and they are designed to fill the gaps in Medicare coverage. There are ten different Medigap plans available, each offering a different level of coverage.

Long-Term Care Insurance: Long-term care insurance can help pay for the cost of long-term care services, such as nursing home care or in-home care. Long-term care insurance policies vary widely in terms of coverage, cost, and eligibility, and it's important to carefully consider your options and choose a policy that fits your needs and budget.

Health Savings Account (HSA): If you have a high-deductible health plan (HDHP), you may be eligible to contribute to a Health Savings Account (HSA). HSAs are tax-advantaged accounts that can be used to pay for healthcare expenses, and the money in an HSA can be invested and grown tax-free.

Retirement Savings: Many people use their retirement savings to pay for healthcare expenses in retirement. This may include funds in a traditional or Roth IRA, a 401(k) plan, or other retirement accounts. While these funds can be used to pay for healthcare expenses, it's important to consider the impact on your overall retirement savings and whether you will have enough money to last throughout your retirement.

Managing Your Retirement Lifestyle

Retirement is the time when you finally get to relax and enjoy the fruits of your labor. However, managing your retirement lifestyle can be challenging if you don't plan. Here are some tips to help you manage your retirement lifestyle:

1. Create a Retirement Budget: Before you can start enjoying your retirement, it's important to create a budget that outlines your expected expenses. This will help you keep track of your income and expenses and ensure that you can meet your financial obligations.

2. Make Smart Investments: Investing your money wisely is key to having enough to live on in retirement. Consider investing in stocks, bonds, mutual funds, and other vehicles that can provide you with a steady stream of income.

3. Make the Most of Your Social Security Benefits: Social Security is an important part of retirement planning. Make sure to research the available benefits and maximize your payments each month.

4. Downsize Your Home: Downsizing your home can be a great way to save money. Consider

downsizing to a smaller house or apartment that fits your current lifestyle and needs.

5. Cut Back on Unnecessary Expenses: Retirement is the perfect time to cut back on unnecessary expenses. Consider reducing your grocery bill and cutting back on entertainment costs.

6. Take Care of Your Health: Taking care of your health is important in retirement. Make sure to eat properly, exercise regularly, and get regular medical check-ups.

7. Stay Active: Retirement is the perfect time to stay active and enjoy your hobbies. Consider joining a gym, taking up a new hobby, or volunteering at a local charity.

8. Stay Connected: Staying connected to friends and family is important. Consider joining a local club, attending church activities, or simply getting together with friends for coffee.

By taking the time to plan and manage your retirement lifestyle, you can ensure that you have enough money to live comfortably and enjoy the rest of your life. With the right plan in place, you can be sure to make the most of your retirement years.

Retirement housing options

Do you choose to stay in your current home, downsize or move elsewhere altogether? Here are some of the most popular retirement housing options to consider.

1. Continuing to Live in your Current Home
Many retirees choose to stay in their current home, especially if it's been paid off. Staying put may make sense for those who have put down roots in their community and are attached to their neighborhood. However, it's important to consider whether living in a large home is practical and cost-efficient. You may need to undertake modifications to make your home more suitable for aging in place, such as installing a stairlift or widening doorways or hallways.

2. Downsizing
Downsizing is a popular choice for retirees looking to reduce their cost of living and simplify their lifestyles. Moving to a smaller home can help reduce your energy bills, home maintenance costs, and the amount of cleaning and upkeep needed. However, you'll need to find a suitable property that meets

your needs and budget, and you may need to part with some of your possessions.

3. Retirement Communities

Retirement communities are designed for people aged 55 and over, and offer a range of housing options and lifestyle amenities. There are plenty of facilities available, from swimming pools and gyms to libraries and cafes. These communities are typically close to medical facilities, shopping centers, and other social activities. However, they may be expensive, depending on the location and facilities offered.

4. Assisted Living Facilities

Assisted living facilities are designed for seniors who need additional support or care. Residents typically have access to 24-hour care and assistance with daily living activities. Staff can provide medication management and other support services. These facilities are often located in secure buildings with restricted access, providing a safe and supportive environment.

5. Nursing Homes

Nursing homes provide 24-hour care and medical support to elderly people who require significant assistance. These facilities are staffed with nurses and other medical professionals and provide a range of medical treatments and therapies. However, nursing homes are typically more expensive than other retirement housing options and may not be suitable for those who are more independent.

Retirement housing is an important decision and one that should not be taken lightly. Consider your lifestyle, budget, and needs when choosing a retirement option. Be sure to research all your options thoroughly before making a decision.

Travel and Leisure Planning

Whether you're retiring in a few months or years, it's important to plan for the best travel and leisure experiences. Here are some tips on how to plan for your retirement travel and leisure.

Do Research: Research is key when it comes to planning for retirement travel and leisure. Find out about different destinations, activities, and attractions that appeal to you and your retirement goals. Research can also help you save money by finding discounts and special offers on travel and leisure.

Set a Budget: Before you start planning for retirement travel and leisure, it's important to set a budget. This will help you determine how much you can afford to spend on travel and leisure activities. It's also important to factor in the cost of transportation and accommodations so that you can make sure the budget works for you.

Prioritize Your Travel Goals: Before you start planning for retirement travel and leisure, it's important to prioritize your travel goals. Think about what type of experiences you are looking for and make a list of places you want to go. This will help you narrow down your options and make the best choices for your retirement travel and leisure.

Explore Local Destinations: Retirement may be the perfect time to explore local destinations. Look for sites and attractions in your area that you may not have had the chance to visit before. This is a great way to get to know your area better and experience the culture.

Consider Your Health: When planning retirement travel and leisure, it's important to consider your health. Make sure that you are physically able to enjoy the activities you have planned. If you have any health concerns, make sure to talk to your doctor before you start planning your travels.

These are just a few tips for retirement travel and leisure planning. By doing your research, setting a budget, prioritizing your travel goals, exploring local destinations, and considering your health, you can ensure that you have the best travel and leisure experiences when you retire.

Voluntary Work and Volunteering

Volunteering and voluntary work are two of the most rewarding and fulfilling activities a person can do during their retirement years. Not only does it provide an opportunity to give back to the community, but it also offers an avenue for socializing, learning new skills, and pursuing hobbies.

Retirees who are looking for a way to stay active and give back to the community can consider volunteering in a variety of ways. They can help out in local schools or churches, mentor or tutor children, or assist with a nonprofit organization's fundraising efforts. There are also opportunities to volunteer with animal shelters, soup kitchens, senior centers, and other charitable organizations.

Volunteering can also be beneficial to retirees in terms of physical health. It can help keep them active and reduce stress levels. Additionally, volunteering offers a sense of purpose and meaning in life, which can be beneficial for people in their later years.

In addition to providing a sense of purpose and meaning in life, volunteering can offer retirees the opportunity to make new friends and gain new skills. For example, a retiree might volunteer to help out at a local animal shelter, where they could learn about animal care and even get to know the animals. They could also volunteer at a senior center, where they could learn about nutrition and health, or even help with computer courses.

No matter how retirees decide to volunteer, it's important to remember that volunteering is a two-way street. Not only does it provide benefits to the community, but it can also provide retirees with a way to stay active and give back to the world around them. With a little bit of research, retirees can find an opportunity that's right for them and make a lasting impact on those in need.

Navigating Retirement Challenges

Retirement can be a difficult transition for many people. After years of hard work and a busy lifestyle, having to suddenly adjust to a much slower pace can be difficult. For those just beginning their retirement journey, it's important to know that there are a variety of challenges they may face and how to navigate them.

One of the biggest challenges of retirement is figuring out how to stay active and engaged. After years of work, many retirees find that their social life has dwindled and they do not have enough activities to fill their days. Retirees need to find activities that keep them busy, such as volunteering, starting a hobby, or just taking a walk each day. Doing something with a purpose can help retirees stay connected and engaged with their community.

Retirees may also face financial challenges. It's important for retirees to understand their retirement income sources, such as Social Security and pension plans, and to plan for any potential gaps in their income. They should also make sure to save for emergency expenses and long-term care. It may be helpful to consult with a financial advisor to review retirement income sources, create a budget and develop a plan for saving.

Another potential challenge is maintaining physical and mental health. After retirement, it can be difficult to stay active and motivated. Retirees need to find activities that keep them physically and mentally fit, such as exercise, joining a class, or taking up a new hobby. It's also important to stay connected with friends and family, as social interaction can have a positive effect on mental health.

Finally, retirees need to have a plan for the future. Retirement is often seen as the end of one's working life, but it is just the beginning of a new chapter. Retirees need to have a plan for what they want to do with their life after retirement, such as travel, pursue a hobby, or start a business. Having a plan can help retirees stay focused and motivated.

Navigating the challenges of retirement can be difficult, but it doesn't have to be. By staying active, planning for finances, and creating a plan for the future, retirees can make the most of their retirement and enjoy their newfound freedom.

Dealing with Inflation

Inflation is an unavoidable reality for retirees. It's the natural result of the rising cost of goods and services due to an increase in demand or a decrease in supply. This increase in cost means your purchasing power decreases over time, as it becomes more expensive to buy the same items.

If you're a retiree, you're likely already facing the challenge of dealing with inflation. But there are steps you can take to protect your retirement income and maintain your purchasing power.

The first step is to invest in inflation-proof assets. These assets, such as stocks and bonds, have a higher rate of return than inflation and can help you stay ahead of inflation. Investing in index funds is a great way to diversify your portfolio and minimize the risk of market downturns.

Another strategy is to diversify your retirement income sources. Having multiple sources of income can help you better manage inflation. Consider combining your Social Security benefits, pension, and other retirement income sources with investments, such as dividend-paying stocks and real estate. By diversifying your income streams, you can protect yourself against the effects of inflation.

You should also consider increasing your contributions to retirement accounts, such as a 401(k) or IRA. By doing so, you'll be able to benefit from compounding returns and make up for any losses from inflation.

Lastly, you can look for ways to cut back on your expenses. This will help you save more money and maintain your purchasing power. Consider downsizing to a smaller home or taking advantage of discounts and rewards programs.

Dealing with inflation in retirement can be difficult, but it's not impossible. With the right strategies and smart investing, you can protect your retirement income and maintain your purchasing power.

Understanding the Impact of Market Volatility

The stock market's ups and downs can have a big impact on your retirement plans. Market volatility can be a scary thing, especially if you are retired or nearing retirement. While it's impossible to predict the future, understanding the basics of market volatility can help you make better decisions and plan for the long term.

Market volatility is simply the measure of how much prices can change over a given period of time. It's a normal part of investing, and while it can create potential returns, it can also create considerable losses. When the market is volatile, the prices of stocks and other securities can swing rapidly, making it difficult to plan for the future.

For retirees, market volatility can have a particularly significant impact. Because most retirees are living off a fixed income, any losses in the stock market can be difficult to recoup. Furthermore, market volatility can reduce the purchasing power of retirement income, as inflation increases the cost of living.

Fortunately, there are a few steps you can take to protect yourself from the effects of market volatility. The first step is to understand the risks associated with investing in the stock market. Generally, the longer you stay invested in the market, the more likely you are to come out ahead, despite temporary dips in prices.

Next, consider diversifying your investments. This means investing in a variety of different stocks, bonds, and other securities, to spread out your risk. This way, if one type of investment takes a downturn, you'll have other investments to cushion the blow.

Finally, consider using a financial advisor. A financial advisor can help you create a portfolio that is tailored to your individual needs and goals. They can also help you develop a retirement plan that takes into account the potential impact of market volatility.

By understanding the basics of market volatility and taking proactive steps to plan for the future, you can minimize the impact of market volatility on your retirement plans. With proper planning and a diversified portfolio, you can ensure a secure financial future.

Managing Debt in Retirement

Retirement is a time to relax and enjoy life, and managing your debt should be a part of that. Many people find themselves managing debt in retirement, and it can be difficult to know what steps to take. With some careful planning and the right strategy, you can manage your debt and still enjoy your retirement.

The first step in managing debt in retirement is to create a budget. A budget will help you track your expenses and income so you can make sure your debt payments are being made on time. Make sure to include all of your retirement income, such as Social Security, pensions, and investments.

Once you know how much income you have coming in each month, you can decide which debts to pay off first. Prioritize your debts according to their interest rates, as the higher-interest debts should be paid off first. Make sure to make at least the minimum payments on all of your debts each month, and if possible, pay more than the minimum.

If you are struggling to make payments, you may want to consider consolidating your debt. Consolidation can help you get a lower interest rate, make one monthly payment, and pay off your debt faster. You may also want to consider refinancing your home if you have equity in it. This can help you lower your interest rate and reduce your monthly payment.

It is also important to remember that debt doesn't just go away. Even if you don't have to make payments on it, it can still affect your credit score. Make sure to keep up with your debt and make payments when you can.

Finally, consider seeking help if you are having difficulty managing your debt. There are many organizations and resources available to help you manage your debt in retirement. They can provide counseling, help you negotiate with creditors, and provide advice on how to better manage your finances.

Managing debt in retirement can be tricky, but with some careful planning and the right strategy, you can still enjoy your retirement and get out of debt. Create a budget, prioritize your debts, and consider options such as debt consolidation and home refinancing. Seek help if you need it, and remember that debt doesn't just go away. With the right approach, you can manage your debt and still have a comfortable retirement.

Working During Retirement

For those who want to continue to stay active and engaged in the working world, working during retirement can be a great option.

The first step in deciding whether to work during retirement is to assess your financial needs. Working during retirement can bring in extra income, which can be beneficial for those who are looking to supplement their retirement savings. It can also help cover expenses such as medical bills or travel costs. Additionally, working during retirement can provide you with a sense of purpose and help you stay connected to the world around you.

If you decide to work during retirement, there are a few things to consider. Firstly, you should think about what type of job you would like to do. Do you want to stay in your current field or try something new? There are plenty of options available, ranging from part-time work to consulting to freelance work. It's important to research these options and find the one that's right for you.

You should also consider the impact that working during retirement may have on your taxes. Some employers may offer tax-advantaged retirement plans, such as 401(k)s or IRAs. Additionally, you may be able to take advantage of the IRS's "catch-up" contribution limit, which allows those over 50 to contribute more than the standard limit to their retirement accounts.

Finally, it's important to be aware of the potential risks associated with working during retirement. For instance, if you're self-employed, you may need to purchase health insurance or other benefits. Additionally, returning to work may mean that you're no longer able to take advantage of certain retirement benefits, such as Social Security.

Working during retirement can be a great way to stay active and engaged in the world. With the right planning and research, it can also be a great way to supplement your retirement income. Just remember to assess your financial needs, consider the type of job you want to do, and understand the potential risks of working during retirement.

Part-Time Jobs and Consulting Work

Part-time jobs and consulting work are becoming increasingly popular options for retirees, offering a flexible way to supplement retirement income and remain engaged in the workforce. Whether you're looking to keep your skills sharp or make some extra money, here's what you need to know about part-time jobs and consulting work for retirees.

Part-time jobs are a great way to stay engaged in the workforce while still having the flexibility to enjoy your retirement. These jobs often involve fewer hours than a full-time job, allowing you to pursue other interests or commitments. Part-time jobs are also often less demanding than full-time positions, allowing you to take on projects or tasks that you find enjoyable.

Consulting work is another great option for retirees who want to stay involved in the workforce. Consulting work typically involves providing advice or expertise in a particular area, such as marketing or accounting. Consulting work is often project-based, allowing you to work on a variety of projects and tasks. Consulting work also offers the potential to make more money than a part-time job, depending on the type of project and the expertise you bring.

When considering part-time jobs or consulting work for retirement, it's important to consider factors such as your skills and experience, the type of work you're interested in, and the amount of time you want to devote to it. You should also think about how this type of work will fit into your retirement plans. For instance, you may want to work part-time to supplement your retirement income or to stay connected to the workforce. Or, you may simply want to pursue a new challenge or stay engaged in an area that you're passionate about.

No matter what type of part-time job or consulting work you decide to pursue, it's important to ensure that you're following all applicable laws and regulations. Consult with a financial advisor or tax specialist to ensure that you're taking all the necessary steps to stay compliant.

Part-time jobs and consulting work can be great options for retirees who want to stay involved in the workforce. These jobs can provide an opportunity to stay connected to the workforce, make some extra money, and pursue activities or tasks that you enjoy. By carefully considering your goals and resources, you can find the right part-time job or consulting work that works for you.

Starting a Business

If you're considering starting a business after retirement, you're not alone. Many retirees are looking for ways to keep busy and earn a little extra money. The good news is that there are plenty of business opportunities for retirees. From consulting to home-based businesses, there are a variety of options available to you.

Before you start a business, you'll need to think about what kind of business you'd like to start. Consider your skills and interests and think about how they could be turned into a business. If you're not sure what type of business you'd like to start, consider consulting services. Consulting services can be a great way to make use of your knowledge and experience.

Once you've decided on the type of business you'd like to start, you'll need to do some research. Find out what the competition is like and what type of customers you'll be targeting. This will help you determine the type of services you'll offer, the pricing structure you'll use, and the marketing strategies you'll employ.

When starting a business after retirement, you'll need to obtain the necessary licenses and permits.

Depending on the type of business you're starting, you may need to apply for a business license, register with the state, and obtain a local business permit. You'll also need to ensure your business and make sure you're up-to-date on all of your taxes.

Finally, you'll need to create a business plan. A business plan will help you define your goals, create a budget, and determine how you will market your business. A business plan will also help you stay organized and on track for success.

Starting a business after retirement can be a great way to stay busy and earn money. With the right planning and preparation, you can be successful in your new venture.

Maximizing Social Security Benefits While Working

Maximizing Social Security benefits while working can be a great way to supplement your income during retirement. The Social Security Administration (SSA) offers a variety of programs and strategies to help you maximize your benefits and get the most out of your retirement years. Here are some tips to help you maximize your Social Security benefits while working:

1. Consider the Earnings Test: The earnings test is a way for the SSA to determine your eligibility for benefits. It includes your gross income and net income, as well as any other sources of income, such as interest, dividends, or capital gains. If your income exceeds certain thresholds, your benefits may be reduced or suspended. Before you decide to work, it's important to understand the earnings test and how it may affect your benefits.

2. Consider the Windfall Elimination Provision: The Windfall Elimination Provision (WEP) is a way for the SSA to reduce benefits for those who are receiving a pension from a job in which they did not pay Social Security taxes. It is important to understand how the WEP affects your benefits before you decide to work.

3. File for Benefits Early: If you're eligible for benefits, it may be beneficial to file for them as early as possible. Filing early will ensure you receive the highest possible benefit amount. However, if you wait until you turn 70 to start receiving benefits, your benefits will be higher than if you had filed earlier.

4. Consider Delaying Benefits: Delaying benefits can be beneficial, especially if you're still working. The longer you wait to start receiving benefits, the higher your monthly benefit amount will be. However, it's important to consider the earnings test before you decide to delay benefits.

5. Utilize Other Retirement Benefits: If you're eligible for other retirement benefits, such as a pension or an IRA, it may be beneficial to utilize them. This can help supplement your Social Security benefits and maximize your total retirement income.

These are just a few tips to help you maximize your Social Security benefits while working. It's important to consider all of your options before deciding what's best for you. The Social Security Administration can provide more information and answer any questions you may have.

Conclusion

Retirement planning is an important part of your financial future. It takes time and effort to create a retirement plan that works for you, but the rewards are worth it. With careful planning and sound investments, you can ensure that you have the financial security in retirement that you desire. By taking the time to create a retirement plan that fits your needs, you can make the most of your retirement years and enjoy financial freedom for the rest of your life.

Final Thoughts on Planning for Retirement

With the right planning, you can ensure that you have enough money to live comfortably in your retirement years. Here are some final thoughts on how to plan for retirement.

First, start early. The earlier you begin to save and invest for retirement, the more time your money has to grow. You can also take advantage of compounding interest, which means that the money you earn will earn interest itself, resulting in bigger returns in the future.

Second, create a budget and stick to it. Setting a budget will help you keep track of your spending and make sure that you have enough money set aside for retirement. You should also consider creating an emergency fund so that you don't have to dip into your retirement savings in case of a financial emergency.

Third, diversify your investments. Different types of investments come with different levels of risk, and you want to make sure that you are spreading out your money over different types of investments. This will help reduce the risk of losing your money in case one of your investments does not perform as well as you had hoped.

Fourth, consider your life expectancy. It is important to think about how long you may live in retirement. This will help you determine how much money you will need to save to maintain your lifestyle throughout your retirement.

Finally, consider getting professional advice. It's always a good idea to have someone knowledgeable look over your retirement plan to make sure that everything is in order. This can help you identify any potential problems or risks that you may not have considered.

Planning for retirement doesn't have to be scary. With the right planning, you can make sure that you have enough money to live comfortably in your retirement years. Just remember to start early, create a budget, diversify your investments, consider your life expectancy, and get professional advice. With these tips, you can be sure to have a secure financial future.

How to Keep Your Retirement Plan on Track

Here are some tips to help you stay on track and reach your retirement goals.
1. Start early. The earlier you start planning for retirement, the easier it will be to reach your goals. Even small contributions can make a huge difference over time, so start as soon as possible.
2. Set realistic goals. It's important to set realistic goals for yourself. Consider your current financial situation, age, income, and other factors when setting your goals.
3. Review your plan regularly. Retirement plans change over time, and it's important to review your plan regularly to make sure it's still on track. Take

into account changes in your life, such as marriage, children, or job changes, to make sure your plan is still relevant.

4. Make sure you're saving enough. Calculate how much money you need to save each month to reach your retirement goals. Remember to account for inflation, as well as any additional money you may need in retirement.

5. Invest wisely. It's important to invest your money wisely. Consider your risk tolerance and goals when selecting investments, and don't be afraid to ask for help if you need it.

6. Utilize tax-advantaged accounts. Retirement accounts such as IRAs and 401(k)s offer tax-advantaged ways to save for retirement. Make sure you're taking advantage of all the benefits these accounts offer.

7. Get professional advice. Consulting a financial advisor can help you stay on track and reach your retirement goals. A financial advisor can provide valuable advice and make sure your plan is still on track.

Retirement planning isn't easy, but with the right strategies, you can keep your plan on track. Start planning as early as possible, set realistic goals, and review your plan regularly. Additionally, make sure you're saving enough, investing wisely, utilizing tax-advantaged accounts, and getting professional advice when needed. By following these tips, you can ensure you're on the right track to reaching your retirement goals.

Where to Find More Resources and Support

To help you find more resources and support for your retirement plan, here are some suggestions.

1. Professional Financial Advisors: Professional financial advisors are trained to provide expert advice on retirement planning. They can help you understand the financial strategies that are best suited to your individual needs, analyze your current financial situation, and recommend retirement options that are best for you.

2. Retirement Planning Books: There are many books available that can provide excellent guidance on retirement planning. These books can help you understand the different types of retirement plans, the tax implications of each, and other factors related to retirement planning.

3. Online Resources: The internet has a wealth of information related to retirement planning. From articles and blogs to calculators and forums, many online resources can help you to plan for retirement.

4. Retirement Organizations: Organizations such as the American Association of Retired Persons (AARP), the National Retirement Planning Coalition (NRPC), and the Retirement Income Industry Association (RIIA) are excellent sources for retirement planning information. They provide resources and support to help you make informed decisions about your retirement plan.

5. Retirement Planning Seminars: Many organizations, universities, and financial institutions offer seminars and workshops on retirement planning. These seminars can provide valuable insights into the different retirement options, the tax implications of each, and other important factors related to retirement planning.

6. Retirement Planning Tools: There are many online tools and calculators available that can help you to plan for retirement. These tools can help you analyze your current financial situation, calculate your future retirement income, and make informed decisions about retirement planning.

7. Financial Institutions: Banks and other financial institutions often provide resources and support for retirement planning. They can provide you with information about different retirement options, help you analyze your financial situation, and recommend the best retirement plan for you.

Retirement planning is an important process. You must take the time to research and understand the different options available to you. Taking advantage of the resources and support available can help you to make informed decisions and ensure a secure financial future.

www.ingramcontent.com/pod-product-compliance
Lightning Source LLC
Chambersburg PA
CBHW050331220526

45465CB00018B/1569